# ROAD MAP FOR LIFE

## SELECTIONS FROM
## ROUTE 365

Toni Sortor and Pamela McQuade

BARBOUR
PUBLISHING

© 2004 by Barbour Publishing, Inc.

ISBN 1-59310-234-8

Cover image © GettyOne, Inc.

Selections are taken from *Route 365—Directions for Life's Journey* by Toni Sortor and Pamela McQuade, © 1999 by Barbour Publishing, Inc.

Published by Barbour Publishing, Inc., P.O. Box 719, Uhrichsville, Ohio 44683, www.barbourbooks.com

*Our mission is to publish and distribute inspirational products offering exceptional value and biblical encouragement to the masses.*

**ecpa** Member of the
Evangelical Christian
Publishers Association

Printed in the United States of America.
5 4 3 2 1

# PREFACE

You've waited a long time for this.

You're on your own, making your way through a great big world full of opportunity, adventure, and challenge.

So what's in store for you now? A job, that's for sure. It may not be the best job in the world, or even close. It might not be what you've "always wanted to do." But you have to start somewhere and begin to build a resume that fills at least one sheet of paper.

How about a place of your own? It probably won't be a palace. In fact, it might be too small and in need of some repairs. But it will be yours, and soon you'll be making plans for moving into a bigger and better place.

This stage of life is exciting, but it may be a lot harder than you ever imagined. For much of your life, you've lived by other people's rules, and even though they were sometimes confining, at least you had some guidelines to live by. Now you have to make your own decisions. Do you spend money faster than you can earn it, snapping up all the latest clothes and electronics? Or do you develop the self-discipline needed to live within your wages and maybe even save a little? Do you spend your free time partying, or do you invest it in volunteer work or classes that will help you get ahead in your career? Do you stop going to church because your parents aren't there to wake you up on Sunday morning, or do you get up and show up on time? The decisions just keep coming.

To make good decisions, you need good information. If you're thinking of buying a particular automobile, you talk to others who own that kind of car and read the reviews in consumer magazines. If you're making a life-changing decision or debating a point of morality, you turn to the one source of good information that will never steer you wrong: the Bible. As God's Word, you can trust it completely.

This book, *Road Map for Life,* will point you to ninety-one key passages in the Bible—passages that deal with the issues you'll face as you're out on your own. This book isn't a replacement for the Bible. But perhaps it can help you through this crucial time and point you in the right direction as you make decisions and choices, both small and large. Get ready for the adventure of your life—and follow Route 365!

*It is not good to have zeal*
*without knowledge, nor to be*
*hasty and miss the way.*

PROVERBS 19:2

You've got dreams and goals and energy to spare. Like a cat locked out of a bedroom, you want to throw yourself against all obstacles. Well, the cat never gets on the bed that way. He doesn't know how to turn the doorknob, after all.

But one night the cat tries another approach. He cries—pitifully, loudly, for minutes on end—and because you love him, you open the door and let him hog the bed. The cat has achieved his goal, hasn't he? He may never learn how to turn a doorknob, but he figured out a way around that problem.

Sometimes, like the cat, you just have to step back and think a problem through. Hitting your head against a door may not do the trick.

**(365)**

*Father, I know what I want out of life, and I'm determined to achieve my goals with Your help. Give me the sense to figure out how to do this with the least possible amount of pain, and if my goals are not pleasing to You, put me on the right track.*

*The fear of the LORD is the beginning of wisdom: a good understanding have all they that do his commandments.*

PSALM 111:10 KJV

We all need to feel we are respected. Unfortunately, respect is hard to earn when you're young. If you haven't been with a company for a few years, almost no one will bother to listen to your good ideas, let alone act on them. Some supervisors will even steal your ideas, taking the credit that rightfully belongs to you! What should you do?

Two paths lead to respect, and the one you choose determines your future—so choose carefully. The first path comes most naturally. You watch your back, strike before you're struck, and butter up the right people until you've clawed your way to the top.

What's the second path? Follow the principles laid down by the Lord. This is not the easy way. It's not a shortcut, and at times it doesn't even seem to work. But it will soon give you self-respect—the first step on the path to success.

365

*Father, help me choose wisely when I come to life's cross-roads. Give me wisdom to choose the Lamb's path, not the tiger's. Help me to be someone who is respected for the way I live, not for the damage I can do.*

*Do not forsake your friend.*

PROVERBS 27:10

One of the saddest days in your life could be the one when you realize things will never be the same again between you and your old friends. You've moved away from the old neighborhood, and so have most of your friends. Besides, you are working different hours, dating or married, and have new interests.

Fight it! Call the parents of your old friends; get phone numbers; then use them. Every time you're in town, look somebody up. Organize a weekend get-together.

Sometimes you'll strike out. A few of the group will drop out of your life totally. Others will have changed so much that you have nothing in common anymore. But a few will respond, and if you keep in touch, keep interested in each other, and spend the necessary time, you will develop new and more mature relationships. It won't be the same as before, but the friendships you cherish can survive. All it takes is one determined person who refuses to let the good times be forgotten.

{365}

*Lord, I know that growth means change, but some things are too good to let die. Help me be the one who keeps us all in touch when life tries to keep us apart.*

*Let no man despise thy youth;
but be thou an example of the
believers, in word, in conversation,
in charity, in spirit, in faith, in purity.*

1 TIMOTHY 4:12 KJV

When someone's referred to as a "good example," most likely that person is middle-aged or older. We tend to look to those who are older than we are for inspiration, figuring they have more experience and wisdom. That is not necessarily true; there are plenty of old fools around.

Don't rule yourself out of the good example population because you're young. Being a good example has nothing to do with age and everything to do with how you live your life. You can be a good example in kindergarten, providing you don't run with scissors.

You don't have to be a Goody Two-shoes, but you should try to live your life with courage and fairness and faith. If you can do that long enough, you're on your way toward becoming a good example. A good reputation opens doors that might otherwise stay closed to you.

**365**

*Lord, I'm not sure I want to be a good example. Maybe for now I'll just concentrate on doing the right thing day by day and see how it works out. Teach me how I should act.*

*How can a young man keep
his way pure? By living
according to your word.*

PSALM 119:9

Finding time to read is hard—but why not dig your copy of the Bible out and put it where you'll see it every day? It has everything you need in it. It has plenty of action and suspense, not to mention memorable characters. If you run into something you don't understand, you can flip the page and find a new subject. If you're dealing with a problem in your life, the answers to it are in the Bible. Plus it can be read in short spurts. You can read a whole psalm while the bread is toasting.

Most importantly, the Bible will teach you how to live according to God's wishes. You can't be a good person without knowing what a good person does. Invest in a concordance, and you'll be able to find everything the Bible says about whatever subject interests you. Then you'll know what God wants you to do. Life does come with an instruction Book.

**365**

*Father, when I have a question about what I should do in a certain circumstance, remind me that all Your answers are there for me in Your Word.*

*But let every man prove his own work,*
*and then shall he have rejoicing in*
*himself alone, and not in another.*
*For every man shall bear his own burden.*

GALATIANS 6:4–5 KJV

Once you graduate and go out into the world, peer pressure lessens, although you will always have some pressure from the groups to which you belong—work groups, church groups, social groups, and so on. At this point in life, though, you have more groups to choose from, and their demands are more moderate, so you have more freedom. You have the chance to "re-invent" yourself. A shy high school student can choose to speak out in a new group. A follower can become a leader, or a leader can decide to take a break.

Now is the time to become the person you've always thought you could be. Carefully choose the groups with whom you want to associate. Assume responsibility for your own actions and take pride in the way you live, "for each one should carry his own load."

(365)

*Lord, now that I have the freedom to be whoever I want to be, help me make wise choices. I want to live a life I can be proud of, and I know You have something special in mind for me.*

> *There are "friends" who destroy*
> *each other, but a real friend sticks*
> *closer than a brother.*

PROVERBS 18:24 NLT

Companions are easier to find than friends. They can be a little wacky, a little wild, a little irresponsible—but you certainly wouldn't want to introduce them to your mother when she comes to visit.

Companions come and go rapidly. They wear out their welcome or decide you've worn out yours, and it's no big deal when you part ways, since no one has any emotional commitment. You've had a few good times, that's all.

Of course, you can't depend on companions for anything. If they're in the mood, they might help you move—once. They may lend you a twenty—once. But when you really need them, they'll be busy.

Fortunately, a few companions become friends. They hang around longer than usual. You find you have several interests in common and begin to talk seriously about deeper, more personal things. If you're really in tune with each other, you invest in each other, although you'd never say something like that. You'll just be there.

We all need friends like this.

**{365}**

*Father, help me to be careful in my choice of companions and willing to be a good friend.*

*And he said, Verily I say unto you, No prophet is accepted in his own country.*

LUKE 4:24 KJV

Jesus knew what many young people have learned through experience: If you want to get ahead in life, you may have to leave your hometown.

Why does it seem easier to get ahead elsewhere? For one thing, everyone knows you too well in your hometown. Even if people remember good things about you, you are still a little boy or girl in their minds, not a competent mechanic or stock market broker.

But not everyone can or wants to leave home. Some work diligently, invest their time and money in their hometowns, and grow in the eyes of their old neighbors until they become town elders themselves. It takes awhile, but the rewards are great, because hometowners love those who do well right where they were planted.

Whether you stay or go is an extremely personal decision. No one knows what you want as well as you do. Ask the Lord to give you guidance, then follow your heart. Besides, this is not an unchangeable decision—you can go home again.

**365**

*Father, You know what I value most in life. Help me sort out my priorities and do what's right for me.*

*I am not writing you a new command*
*but one we have had from the beginning.*
*I ask that we love one another.*
*And this is love:*
*that we walk in obedience to his commands.*

2 JOHN 5–6

Sometimes being a Christian gets confusing. Pressures bear down, and your love grows cold. Spiritual winter sets in. So you start looking for something you've missed, some new trick to alter your life.

The truth is, you probably don't need a trick. You just need to get a handle on the old truth that's stared you in the face for a long time. Then you need to obey what you know.

When your love for God grows cold, take a fresh look at what He's already said. Draw close to the fire of His Word, and your life will alight.

When the cold, dull days of winter make you feel dull, too, renew your love for God. Warm yourself at the Scripture just as you'd seek the heat of a fireplace.

(365)

*Jesus, I already know so much about You, but sometimes I don't use that knowledge in my life. Help me bridge the gap between my head and heart.*

*"These are the words of the
Son of God. . . . I know your deeds,
your love and faith, your service
and perseverance, and that you are
now doing more than you did at first."*

REVELATION 2:18–19

"If I'd known what I was getting into," Rita exclaimed to her pastor, "I never would have become Danielle's friend. I tried to help her out of her troubles, and all she can do is complain!"

Maybe you too have done a good turn—you gave someone a ride, only to have her constantly call whenever she wanted to go to the store, or you gave him advice that backfired. You did good with the best intentions, but now you wish you'd never done it.

When your good deeds seem to haunt you, know that God sees beyond the situation into your heart. He knows you desired only good. He'll bless you for that desire.

Though you experienced bad side effects from your good deeds, never again helping anyone isn't an option. Turn to the One who knows your deeds and do another good deed—chances are it won't backfire.

**(365)**

*Lord, I know every good deed doesn't fall apart. Help me to reach out to others, even when things don't go the way I'd like.*

*Ho, every one that thirsteth, come ye to the waters,*
*and he that hath no money; come ye, buy, and eat;*
*yea, come, buy wine and milk without money*
*and without price. Wherefore do ye spend money*
*for that which is not bread? and your labour*
*for that which satisfieth not?*

ISAIAH 55:1–2 KJV

Payday!" Jim shouted to his roommate. "Can't wait to get that CD player! I'll stop at the store on my way home—and oh, baby, will it blast tonight! Maybe I'd better pick up a couple of CDs too."

Problem was, Jim didn't have the money to buy the equipment. He'd gotten into debt with the store, which charged him an exorbitant interest rate. Already, the apartment stretched Jim's budget, but it didn't seem to matter. When he was short on cash, Jim just played the music louder.

One day Jim couldn't pay the rent, and his roommate got on his case. That night the CD player blared with a new CD.

But a new CD player, new CDs, and all the noise in the world couldn't make Jim happy. Things never solve problems, because they can't fill inner emptiness or bring lasting joy. The high from a buy only lasts a short time.

Invest instead in the joy-bringer—Jesus.

⟨365⟩

*Lord, You know the things I need. Don't let me become a spendaholic when only You can satisfy my deepest desires.*

*A king rejoices in servants who
know what they are doing; he is
angry with those who cause trouble.*

PROVERBS 14:35 NLT

On your way to work, your car suddenly gives you trouble. You know it's practically hung together with rubber bands, but why did it have to break down now? Finally you call a towing service or find a garage.

While you wait for service, do you worry about the work piling up on your desk? Or perhaps you're thinking of the grief your boss will give you when you finally do get in. If you have a long wait, your blood may simmer.

The mechanic's attitude makes a huge difference. If he's helpful and tries to get you on the road quickly, your blood pressure drops again. But if his attitude says, "I'll get to it when I can," you may be furious when you leave—and you won't come to that unwise businessman again.

Every day, you're like that mechanic. You can give God good, positive service or surly responses. Are you a servant He looks forward to using?

{365}

*I want to be a wise servant who glorifies You, Lord, not one with an attitude that reflects badly on You. Keep me diligent in my labors.*

*Then I heard the voice of the Lord
saying, "Whom shall I send? And
who will go for us?" And I said,
"Here am I. Send me!"*

ISAIAH 6:8

Ever wish that you could rewrite that verse to say, "Here am I. Send someone else"? When you feel overloaded spiritually, even though you'd like to comply, opening yourself to full obedience to God is hard.

*Maybe*, you worry, *if I give Him free rein, He'll send me to Timbuktu* (or wherever your least-favorite place in the world is). *How could I ever cope with that?* you wonder.

If you're feeling overloaded, take your burden to God and confess that you've been hanging on to it. Then drop it in His hands and run! Don't stick around to pull it back out of the hands of the great burden lifter.

Then let Him lead you as you make decisions about ministries with which you're overinvolved, family problems that someone else needs to handle, or commitments you may not need to take on.

Pledge yourself to obedience, and walk in your new freedom. Don't let that old burden trap you again!

*Send me, Lord, wherever You want me to go. I know You'll give me the strength I need.*

17

*Come unto me,*
*all ye that labour and are heavy laden,*
*and I will give you rest.*

MATTHEW 11:28 KJV

When you start on heavy labor—helping a friend move into his new place or digging in a garden—you work freely. It seems easy. But as you begin to tire, you set a goal: I'll do this much, then take a rest. Later, your muscles feel the strain, and thoughts of a break fill your mind. Finally, you just have to stop working. It's the same with emotional or spiritual work. You can't go on forever without Jesus' rest.

When you're working forty hours a week, hitting the mall after work, involved in ministry, and visiting friends on the weekend, by the time you get home, you're exhausted. Your Bible sits unused on your nightstand. Next morning, you scramble to the office, and a quiet time just doesn't seem to fit in.

*Life's too hectic,* you think.

Well, of course it is! You missed the first part of this verse and didn't come to Jesus.

**(365)**

*Lord, each day I need to come to You in prayer and through the Scriptures. When I'm feeling too busy, draw me with Your Spirit. I need to schedule a meeting with You.*

*And the sun stood still, and the moon stayed,*
*until the people had avenged*
*themselves upon their enemies. . . .*
*So the sun stood still in the midst*
*of heaven, and hasted not to*
*go down about a whole day.*

JOSHUA 10:13 KJV

Amazing—at a time when they needed it, God gave Israel an extra full day of light! The sun and the moon cooperated with humanity's need, because God declared it.

We can't explain how it happened. Used to the regular rising of the sun and moon, we can't imagine things any other way—and it must have also astonished the Amorites, whom Israel was attacking. Instead of getting away under the cover of night, they had to keep fighting.

Today we have an extra day that only comes once every four years. Unlike the Amorites, we don't get it as a total surprise.

How do we use this extra twenty-four hours? Will it be a blessing to us and others or something that's just lost in the sauce of another year?

Every day is important. God doesn't have to stop time to make it so.

How will you use today?

**365**

*Thank You, Lord, for another day to serve You. I want to make the most of it by showing someone Your love.*

> *"But as for you,*
> *be strong and do not give up,*
> *for your work will be rewarded."*

2 CHRONICLES 15:7

How do you know what God wants you to do? If you think you know, how can you be sure you're not acting out of your own desires instead of God's? Sometimes God seems to be pushing you one way; the next day you feel as if you're on your own.

Doing God's will is a long-term project. You may start out in one direction and get sidetracked. A roadblock may suddenly appear ahead of you, forcing a detour you didn't expect. A door of opportunity you never knew existed may open right in front of you. Our paths seem to travel more like a sailboat than a powerboat. We tack from one direction to another, not making much forward progress.

Eventually you'll know where you're going. Your road will suddenly feel right, and you'll see signs of your destination on the horizon. So tack if you have to, but never give up seeking to do God's will for your life.

**365**

*Father, thank You for the guidance You give me. Although my progress may seem slow, I know You will get me where I'm supposed to be.*

*"He repays a man for what he has done;*
*he brings upon him what*
*his conduct deserves."*

JOB 34:11

God's rewards vary from person to person. There isn't one big, specific reward we are all competing for, which makes sense, since all our hopes and dreams are different, and so are what we consider to be good rewards.

Sometimes God doesn't just hand us our rewards —we have to find them. It's not that God is playing games with us. He just knows that a little effort on our part will make us appreciate our rewards all the more. So the next time your life seems to be all work and no fun, look under a few bushes and discover the surprises God has waiting for you.

🛡365

*O Lord, You care for every part of my life and know me inside out. Although some of my rewards may be hidden right now, I am confident You will help me find them.*

*With the tongue we praise our Lord and Father,*
*and with it we curse men,*
*who have been made in God's likeness.*
*Out of the same mouth come praise and cursing.*
*My brothers, this should not be.*

JAMES 3:9–10

Most of us speak before thinking. It's automatic, out of our control—or so it seems. We use words today that our mothers would have washed our mouths out for using. Stand-up comedians and movie characters use these words so often that they lose all their meaning and eventually fail to shock us at all.

But the phrase "dirty mouth" has a real meaning. Would you take communion with filthy hands? Of course not. It would be sacrilegious. Would you pick up a toddler and tell him a dirty joke? You wouldn't think of it. And yet we take our dirty mouths to church and sing God's praises with them!

If we are going to try to be holy, we have to be aware of what we say, as well as what we do.

365

*Lord, help me gain control of my tongue, so others who hear what I say will be drawn to You and not be put off by my thoughtless words.*

*Take heed, and beware of
covetousness: for a man's life
consisteth not in the abundance
of the things which he possesseth.*

LUKE 12:15 KJV

A bundance of possessions isn't a big problem for a young person starting off. Lack of possessions is much more likely to be the problem. A person isn't being greedy when he wants a car to get to work or a new suit for a job interview, but if the car has to be a Mercedes and the suit Italian made, that's edging into greediness.

In the same way, wanting to succeed is not greed. Ambition is God's way of prodding us into action. But devoting yourself to success day and night, forsaking everything else in the climb to the top—well, that's greed.

As Jesus said, there are all kinds of greed to watch out for. Sometimes it's hard to tell when you've gone over the line. The next time you think you may be falling into greediness, give yourself the "tombstone test." How do you want to be remembered?

**365**

*Father, help me distinguish between ambition and greed. Show me the right choices in how to use my talents and blessings.*

23

*The LORD is nigh unto them that
are of a broken heart; and saveth
such as be of a contrite spirit.*

PSALM 34:18 KJV

You don't hear people talking about broken hearts these days, unless you are fond of country music, but they still happen to everyone at least once. You get dumped by someone you were seriously considering taking home to meet the folks. How could you have misread all the signals? How could something that seemed so good turn out to be a nightmare? What did you do?

Most of us turn into hermits for awhile, dissecting the failed relationship over and over, trying to figure out what happened. Fortunately, friends put an end to that pretty soon, the unromantic fools. They drag you out of the apartment—or sit in it with you until you go out in self-defense. They tell you to get on with your life, and they fix you up with someone new. They nag you back into emotional health.

At the same time, God's doing a little work on you, too. Unlike your friends, He doesn't nag or fix you up with someone new. He's just there for you when you need Him, and He always understands.

(365)

*Father, thank You for comforting me when I go and get my heart broken. I know if it happens again, You'll be there for me as You always are.*

*There hath no temptation taken you*
*but such as is common to man:*
*but God is faithful,*
*who will not suffer you to be tempted*
*above that ye are able;*
*but will with the temptation*
*also make a way to escape,*
*that ye may be able to bear it.*

1 CORINTHIANS 10:13 KJV

Temptations come in all sizes and shapes, from the seven deadly sins to sneaking a second dessert when you're home alone. As the verse above says, temptation is common, and God has seen them all. Even Jesus was tempted. It's not the temptation that makes you a sinner—you have to give in to the temptation to earn that label—and God is still in control of how much temptation comes your way. Better yet, as you begin to waver, He can show you how to get out of the situation. So the next time you are tempted to do something you don't want to do (or something you do want to do), thank God for His help and look for the solution He has provided for you.

**365**

*Father, thank You for Your care whenever I'm tempted. I know I will never be tempted beyond what I can bear. You will give me the strength to resist.*

*"I have labored to no purpose;*
*I have spent my strength in vain and for nothing.*
*Yet what is due me is in the LORD's hand,*
*and my reward is with my God."*

ISAIAH 49:4

Some days you just can't win. The suit you just got back from the cleaner has mud on the cuff. Your cat turned over the goldfish bowl and ate the body. You said something at work, and the silence that followed made you want to creep under a desk. Nothing went right all day.

Doesn't anyone care that you had a rotten day and need a little encouragement? Well, you could call home and get some sympathy, but then you'd have to explain why you haven't been home for three months.

Why not just talk it out with God? He listens without comment. He knows exactly what kind of day you had, and He weeps for you. He's there, and He cares.

*Even if no one seems to appreciate me, I know that You do, Lord. In just a second, my day can become holy when I reach out to You.*

*I am on the verge of collapse, facing constant pain.*
*But I confess my sins;*
*I am deeply sorry for what I have done.*

PSALM 38:17–18 NLT

Jesus was the only perfect person in the world. David, who wrote the verses above, was as sinful as the next man, yet God favored him over all other kings and chose his descendants to be the earthly ancestors of Jesus.

God knows we will sin. It's in our nature to do so. Not that we can use that as an excuse, but it is a fact of life we have to live with. God meant for us to live happy lives, not be weighed down by an unnatural burden of sin. Jesus has accepted that burden for us. Give it over to Him, accept His sacrifice with joy, go on with your life, and try to sin no more.

365

*Father, thank You for forgiving all my sins through Your Son, Jesus Christ. Let me dwell on what You have done for me, not on the many ways I have failed You.*

*One generation will commend your works to another;*
*they will tell of your mighty acts.*
*They will speak of the glorious splendor of your majesty,*
*and I will meditate on your wonderful works.*

PSALM 145:4–5

There was no Internet in the days of David, no instant communication. Most people couldn't read or write. Traditions were taught to a young generation by the older generation, often through stories, songs, and dances, which were memorable and enjoyable ways to learn. The psalms and hymns of the church not only lift people's spirits but serve as teaching tools.

Perhaps you were not cut out to be a witness. The thought of speaking to another person about your beliefs may scare you into silence. But there are other ways to communicate. Can you tell stories? Can you sing? Can you dance? Can you draw? Faith, and the joy it brings you, can be communicated through many means. Offer God the talents you do have, and He will find a way to use them.

365

*Father, show me how I can tell others about Your mighty works and pass on the faith I treasure. You know what I am capable of, and I do want to help.*

*Some men came down from Judea
to Antioch and were teaching the
brothers: "Unless you are circumcised,
according to the custom taught by Moses,
you cannot be saved."*

ACTS 15:1

**P**eople—even some well-meaning Christians—
have a hard time accepting grace. They can't believe they don't have to add something to God's
work. So they set up rules and regulations: "You have
to do this, or you aren't a Christian." "You don't really
love God unless you do that."

The men in this verse were trying to follow the
Old Testament Law as well as Jesus. They couldn't
accept that His blood had done it all and that, when
they accepted Him, their hearts, not their bodies,
were circumcised. Many serious Gentile believers who
wanted to obey God and feared setting a foot wrong
did what these Judaizers said. Fear led them into sin.

God doesn't want you to be afraid, to worry if
you've dotted all the i's and crossed all the t's that will
let you enter heaven.

No, He loved you, so He gave you a free gift, no
strings attached. Enjoy that gift today.

(365)

*Thank You, Jesus, for Your grace. You've done everything
that had to be done to bring me into heaven. I want to
give my life as thanks.*

*Therefore, among God's churches*
*we boast about your perseverance*
*and faith in all the persecutions*
*and trials you are enduring.*

2 THESSALONIANS 1:4

Paul commended the Thessalonian Christians on their powerful faith, which had become the talk of the Christian world. The apostle boasted about them wherever he went.

*Sure,* you may be thinking, *I could be like that if I lived back then. It was easier for them.*

We'd like to think that. When our own witness seems weak, we assume others have it easier than we do. We excuse ourselves, *If only I had this. . .* Or, *If only I were older. . .* The *if onlys* could go on endlessly.

But the Thessalonians weren't armchair Christians. They suffered and endured trials. Many must have felt that being Christian wasn't always worth it.

*Do we have to struggle so much?* both we and the Thessalonians have wondered. *If only God would make our lives easier, couldn't we have a better witness?* we ask.

But trials and troubles are the tools God uses to develop His greatest saints.

Hold fast today!

**365**

*Lord, some days the trials come raining down on me. No matter what my situation, let me be faithful to You.*

*Commit your way to the LORD;*
*trust in him and he. . .*
*will make your righteousness shine like the dawn.*

PSALM 37:5–6

Even the laziest couch potato discovers energy after seeing one of those pricy fitness machines. They offer visions of a new, sleeker you.

But once you try out these tempting machines, you learn it takes commitment and consistency to get that new figure. Before long, the machine becomes a place to drop your coat—but a clothes rack would have cost a whole lot less.

Coming to Jesus is something like buying exercise equipment. All you need to be successful is right there, ready to be used. But your Christian testimony won't automatically shine out in a dark world. That takes daily commitment and trust in God. Righteousness needs to be built up day by day.

Some people's Christian walk never goes further than their stroll down the aisle during an altar call. They don't want to change their lives. Those people are expensive clothes racks.

Seek out God every day through prayer, fellowship, and His Word, and you'll become a truly fit Christian.

*Lord, I don't want to be useless to You. Make me fit for Your kingdom.*

*"This poor widow has put more
into the treasury than all the others.
They all gave out of their wealth;
but she, out of her poverty, put in
everything—all she had to live on."*

MARK 12:43–44

Doesn't part of you wish you were as brave as the widow who dropped her last coins into the temple treasury? *How would I live if I gave that much?* you probably ask yourself. *What would I do?* Scary, isn't it?

Scripture doesn't tell us the widow went home to find money waiting for her. We can't guarantee that the story had that kind of happy ending.

But we know that, whatever happened, God knew what she had done and blessed her. Doesn't He promise to bless those who give?

Faith often means hanging on the edge, not knowing all the answers. Maybe for you it isn't putting your last pennies in the offering plate, but it's putting a tithe in when you don't know how you'll pay that last bill. Or maybe it's sharing the gospel with someone, when you don't know if he'll object.

That's life on the edge of faith.

(365)

*Lord, I don't want to be so comfortable that I forget what life's like on the edge. Make my faith walk exciting.*

*It is of the LORD's mercies
that we are not consumed,
because his compassions
fail not. They are new every
morning: great is thy faithfulness.*

LAMENTATIONS 3:22–23 KJV

Troubles seemed to overflow Craig. He spent more and more time on the job as his boss loaded him with work. His mom went into the hospital for tests. His girlfriend disappeared from his life. The pastor of his church resigned, and Craig wondered if anything in life was stable. Troubles seemed to eat Craig up inside.

Life's challenges can hit us hard—and suddenly. One moment you have one problem you're dealing with, and the next you have three or four. *Has God forgotten me? Will He leave me stranded?* you may wonder.

Never. Compassion is God's "middle name." Every day, even the lousy ones, He remains faithful. You may not see the way He's working, but He's out ahead, protecting you.

No trouble can eat you up when you belong to God. It may nibble at your edges, but you won't be consumed.

(365)

*Lord, faith isn't just emotions. When I get that empty, stranded feeling, I know it's nothing You put in my heart. I don't want to be eaten up with worry—just consumed with Your Word.*

*" 'Give us each day our daily bread.' "*

LUKE 11:3

Getting caught up in a round of chores—laundry, cleaning, and shopping—isn't very exciting. But the work has to get done sometime, and even the worst housekeeper has to spend some time doing it.

*Surely God can't have a purpose in this,* we think. *There's nothing crucial to His kingdom here.*

Does God know you have to go to the cleaners, wash the car, and buy food? Of course He does. Our need for "daily bread"—and meat, and eggs, and even clean laundry—doesn't come as a surprise to Him. He provides for it all.

But in the midst of our busyness, we need to keep time for God. We can start the day with devotions, encourage a friend who phones just as we pick up a sponge to clean the bathroom, and reach out to someone in front of us in line at the grocery store.

Even dull days become exciting when you serve the Lord of the universe.

**365**

*Lord, even days that don't seem to make great gains for Your kingdom are ordained by You. Help me touch others today.*

*"Teach them the decrees and laws,
and show them the way to live and
the duties they are to perform."*

EXODUS 18:20

Everyone new to a job needs to be taught what to do and how to do it. You have to ask some pretty stupid questions before you can even start your work. Even flipping a burger can be done in a number of ways, only one of which will be the "right" way. Then, once you get the procedures down pat, you'll go and violate some unwritten law that nobody ever mentioned. How are you supposed to learn all this stuff on your own?

You can't—at least not fast enough to avoid some serious goofs. You have to take notice of all these little things while you work, juggling everything at once. If you're fortunate, you'll find someone willing to give you some clues until you can handle it all alone. Treasure this kind soul. Then, when you're experienced and savvy, take a new hire under your wing and return the favor.

**365**

*Lord, give me the patience I need to learn all the written and unwritten rules of my job. Give me one friend I can trust to fill me in, and I will do the same for another in the future.*

*We must pay more careful attention, therefore,*
*to what we have heard,*
*so that we do not drift away.*

HEBREWS 2:1

All your life, Mom and Dad have taken responsibility for getting you to church, but that's over now. You may live miles from them or in the same town, but except for a little nagging, they can't control your actions anymore. It's on your head if you don't get yourself to church.

There are all kinds of excuses you can use, from not being able to find a friendly congregation to not feeling the need for church. It's easy to drift away, once your old habits have been broken and you're living in a new situation.

But Sunday's not the same without church. There's something nice missing from your week, even if you can't pinpoint it. Maybe Mom and Dad were right, and you need to pay more careful attention to what you have heard—from them and the Lord. Maybe it's time to find that friendly congregation and admit that you need to go to church.

**⟨365⟩**

*Father, it's so easy to drift away from old habits, even the good ones. Help me remember the warmth of fellowship, the security of being part of a congregation, and my need for You.*

*Remember now thy Creator in
the days of thy youth, while the
evil days come not, nor the years
draw nigh, when thou shalt say,
I have no pleasure in them.*

ECCLESIASTES 12:1 KJV

Right now is one of the best times of your life. You are young and strong, unafraid of the future, and eager to experience all that life will bring. Now is the time to remember your Creator and thank Him for everything He has given you. Now is the time to enjoy yourself, sing His praises, and keep His commandments.

Remember how you used to thank your mom when she gave you your favorite food for dinner or took you on a great vacation? You thanked her with your whole heart and happily obeyed her rules. The days she gave you Brussels sprouts, you undoubtedly did not thank her—or take the garbage out without complaining. It works the same way in your relationship with God. Now, while things are going well, be lavish in your thanks, because it will be harder to do as life gets harder.

**365**

*Father, thank You for the joys of life I see all around me today. Teach me now, while I am still young, how to live in a way that pleases You.*

*By faith Abraham, when called
to go to a place he would later
receive as his inheritance, obeyed
and went, even though he did not
know where he was going.*

HEBREWS 11:8

L ife rarely turns out as you planned. Oh, you can
sit down and list your life goals for the next five
or ten years. This is actually a good idea, because it
helps you focus on your priorities. Just don't be sur-
prised when you look back five or ten years later and
see how far off the mark you've strayed.

This doesn't mean you shouldn't plan. Some of
the best things in your life will come to you because
of planning. But some of the best things will also
come without planning for them at all. That's what
makes life so much fun. It's a daily surprise, and you
need to stride into it with faith, even if you don't
know where you're going.

**(365)**

*Father, I know You will provide what's best for me, even
if I don't understand at the time. Let me walk in faith,
like Abraham, confident that You know my path better
than I do.*

> *"Who of you by worrying can add
> a single hour to his life?"*
>
> MATTHEW 6:27

With a closet full of clothes, we worry about not having the right thing to wear. With a cupboard full of food, there's still nothing to eat. These are minor worries not based on fact, but they continue to nag at us until we go out and buy the "right" clothes or cram the cupboard with enough food to feed a small nation.

Many people have more legitimate worries—actual needs that consume every waking moment in a struggle for survival. What's amazing is that many of these people are still happy, despite their problems. How do they do it? Perhaps they've read a little further in Matthew 6, where Jesus promised, " 'Seek first his kingdom and his righteousness, and all these things will be given to you as well' " (verse 33).

Worry wastes time because it produces nothing, while seeking God and His kingdom is always a worthwhile activity that will banish trivial worries and provide us with whatever we need.

### 365

*Father, I know the rent money will be there when I need it if I concentrate on living righteously and don't let my worries paralyze me. Times may get tough, but I can make it with Your help.*

*Young man,*
*it's wonderful to be young!*
*Enjoy every minute of it.*

ECCLESIASTES 11:9 NLT

This verse ends, "but know that for all these things God will bring you to judgment." Doesn't the ending of this verse contradict the beginning? Wouldn't it make more sense to forego the happiness to be safe during the judgment?

No, it would be foolish to live that way. A Christian should enjoy life, and youth is the time to enjoy it to its fullest. A good person does not have to walk around avoiding all fun just to be safe. Those who do so lead lonely, unfulfilling lives, which is certainly not what God had in mind for the faithful.

What this verse is saying is that there are some limits you'll have to be aware of while you're having fun. Some activities are inappropriate for the faithful. But you know that, and you know it's perfectly possible to enjoy living the faithful life. Don't wrap yourself up in "thou shalt nots" and deny yourself all the fun God means you to enjoy.

**(365)**

*Father, show me the limits I need to know, but help me lead a happy, fulfilling life at the same time, a good witness of Your love.*

*How long, O LORD, must I call*
*for help, but you do not listen?*
*Or cry out to you, "Violence!"*
*but you do not save?*

HABAKKUK 1:2

We'd like to think believers never suffer serious, long-term wrongs. All Christians' troubles should be minor ones; after all, don't we serve God?

When we think this way, we've created a god who's almost at our beck and call. We're acting as if we're favored ones to whom He caters.

God didn't save us to place us in an ivory tower, apart from the miseries of this world. He didn't do that to Jesus, and He won't do it for us. Anyone who's been a Christian for long can tell you we don't always get instant prayer answers. Like Habakkuk, we'll find our faith tested by a long wait.

But at the end of God's delays, He often does something greater than anything we expected. Though His response may take days, weeks, or years, it comes at the right time.

Don't limit His work in your life by failing to pray.

(365)

*Jesus, You're Lord of my life, not my personal slave. Help me to seek Your will in prayer.*

*I have set before you life and death,*
*blessing and cursing: therefore choose life,*
*that both thou and thy seed may live:*
*That thou mayest love the LORD thy God,*
*and that thou mayest obey his voice,*
*and that thou mayest cleave unto him.*

DEUTERONOMY 30:19–20 KJV

You're moving into a new life. As you graduate, a whole world sits out there to discover.

But it's a big world. Looking at the decisions you'll face and the things that could go wrong, you may feel scared.

Life's made up of a lot of decisions—do I move here, take that job, go along with the program or break away from it? More importantly, life is made up of moral choices that have even more impact on your future.

Bad moral choices can spell death for relationships, but good ones bring them new life. Choices close opportunities to you (after all, who wants to hire a thief?) or open up new vistas.

If you're really into the Word, you know what those right choices are. They're all in the Book. Put them to work in your life, and you'll be blessed!

**(365)**

*When I read Your Word, I see the things I should do. Give me strength, Lord, to follow through with right choices.*

*Worship the LORD with gladness;*
*come before him with joyful songs.*

PSALM 100:2

Some music sounds good to you—and some is just an irritating noise. But you've probably found out that your "noise" is another person's "sounds good."

Church music is part of the "noise"–"sounds good" debate. If your congregation likes the "oldies and moldies" of Christian music and you like the latest tunes on the Christian music shelves, you may be tempted to hold your ears during services. Worse, those slow, dull songs may lull you to sleep.

Chances are the music you can't stand is favored by your pastor or music leader. Maybe other church members have encouraged the music director to play it. Asking anyone to change it could start World War III.

This psalm doesn't mention the kind of music churches should play—it doesn't specify classical, pop, rock music, or even Old Testament-style music. That's because the music isn't important—worshipping God is. He deserves our praise, no matter what the song is. A joyful heart can always praise Him.

Whether or not your church is tuned in to your music style, sing with all your heart.

(365)

*Lord, I want to praise You, not start a war. Thank You for music I enjoy. Let me sing Your praises today.*

*"My intercessor is my friend*
*as my eyes pour out tears to God;*
*on behalf of a man he pleads with God*
*as a man pleads for his friend."*

JOB 16:20–21

How do you pray for others? Is it merely, "Bless John, bless Jane"? Imagine yourself in God's shoes, listening to such a shopping list of prayer. Pretty boring, isn't it?

Hearing such stuff must be harder for Him than praying it is for us. God's heart breaks when He thinks of all the blessings we could ask for that He would gladly give. But if He gave what we asked, what would that be? Are we looking for healing, peaceful relationships, conversion, or a thousand other things?

We'll never quite know how prayer works to move God's hand. But through the Spirit, who intercedes for us, we can bring the needs of friends, family, and even Christians who live half a world away to the Father. Lives begin to change, and we can praise God for His works.

The Spirit intercedes for you every day. Are you interceding for others, too?

(365)

*Father God, fill me with Your love for others. Let my prayer time be a blessing to the world.*

*Love is patient, love is kind.*
*It does not envy, it does not boast, it is not proud.*

1 CORINTHIANS 13:4

If you're involved in a special romance, do you treat your beloved as someone who's exciting to be around? Probably. But do you also show your honey God's love by living out this verse?

Dating relationships can make emotions run high, but if you're constantly impatient with a date who's never on time or are unkind to one who's having a tough time seeing eye-to-eye with a family member, you're not reflecting God's love.

God doesn't rewrite the Book so we can act any way we want in our romances. Nowhere does God say we have a right to treat the ones closest to our hearts with less respect than a chance acquaintance or a close friend. When we really love, we treat each other with extraspecial gentleness and care.

If you can't treat a date with patience, kindness, and trust, reevaluate things. Your spiritual walk may be slipping. Or perhaps this isn't a person you're suited to, and you'd be better off as "just friends."

**365**

*Lord, help me show Your love to anyone I date. Don't let me make my romantic life an exception to Your rules.*

*When times are good, be happy;*
*but when times are bad, consider:*
*God has made the one as well as the other.*
*Therefore, a man cannot*
*discover anything about his future.*

You can't predict the future. You can only plan to the best of your ability and move forward in faith.

So decide what kind of career you want. Work hard at it. But stay open to new ideas and truths along your path to success. Likewise, stay open to finding the mate God has for you, but don't put on a pith helmet and go hunting for one, or you'll turn romance away.

Despite all your good strategies, you'll run into a few roadblocks. Maybe your first career won't be as enjoyable as you'd expected, and you'll go back to school. Or you might wait a few extra years to meet Mr. or Ms. Right. But delays or detours don't have to end your trip.

Even your worst times aren't out of God's control. His master plan can't be circumvented. So enjoy the good days and know that the really bad ones can still lead you closer to God.

Take each day as it comes—a gift from Him.

**365**

*Whether today is great or out of control, I trust in You, Lord.*

*Whose adorning let it not be that*
*outward adorning of plaiting the hair,*
*and of wearing of gold, or of putting on of apparel;*
*But let it be the hidden man of the heart,*
*in that which is not corruptible,*
*even the ornament of a meek and quiet spirit,*
*which is in the sight of God of great price.*

1 PETER 3:3–4 KJV

Some people would look great dressed in anything, with no makeup. The rest of us need a little help—and there's nothing wrong with looking your best. A few hours a week in the gym will not only tighten up your waistline but also leave you healthier and happier. A new dress or suit may make you more confident.

On the other hand, we all know perfectly gorgeous people whose souls live in a swamp. You may admire their appearance but wouldn't trust them to walk your dog. Their beauty is skin-deep—or less.

In the long run, it's performance that counts, which is exactly what this verse is saying. Do what you can with your outer self, but concentrate on the "unfading beauty of a gentle and quiet spirit."

🛡365🛡

*Lord, I will never be one of the beautiful people the world seems to favor, but I can develop the kind of inner beauty that You prefer. Thank You for judging me on the basis of how I live, not how I look.*

> *"Seek the peace and prosperity of the city*
> *to which I have carried you into exile.*
> *Pray to the LORD for it,*
> *because if it prospers, you too will prosper."*

JEREMIAH 29:7

Our hearts always know where our home is, especially if we're not living there. Although we may yearn to be elsewhere, we have to make do with where we are. We never have to give up the dream of returning home someday, but we do have to live in the present, and it is wise to invest in our current home. Making this town a better place to live is to our own advantage, both psychologically and financially.

Have you registered to vote in your current location? Have you found a church to attend, a doctor, and a dentist? Do you shop locally or put off buying what you need until you return to your "real" home? Do you do volunteer work? Have you made some local friends? It may be decades before you can live in the place your heart calls home. Don't waste years dreaming of somewhere else when you can contribute where you are now.

365

*Father, show me how I can help out wherever I'm living right now.*

*"For I know the plans I have for you," says the LORD.
"They are plans for good and not for disaster,
to give you a future and a hope."*

JEREMIAH 29:11 NLT

We all have plans for our future, even if they're a little vague. We know whether we want to marry and have children, places we want to go, and things we hope to accomplish. Most of us are realistic about our plans, knowing some will work out and some won't. We also know our plans will change from year to year as we mature and see more of the world.

What we don't like is to have our plans blown out of the water and to have our lives take a sudden change of direction. There's nothing more frightening than losing the anchor that's been holding our life in place and being forced to start over again.

Fortunately, some of these disasters turn out to be blessings. Even when we have no idea which way to turn, the Lord knows where we're going and will keep us on the right path, even if the trip's a little bumpy.

365

*Father, when my life suddenly turns upside down, I will trust in You to lead me in the right direction.*

*They think it strange that you do not plunge with them*
*into the same flood of dissipation,*
*and they heap abuse on you.*

1 PETER 4:4

Some graduates go a little crazy once they're free of parental limits. If Dad's not around to smell their breath at the front door, they think drinking to excess is perfectly acceptable. Mom's not standing at the foot of the stairs, so it must be okay to take a date to their room. The moral police aren't in residence anymore.

It's true—they aren't. No one is going to impose moral behavior on you, short of criminal acts. You're on your own. It's a learning experience we all have to go through, and some can't handle the sudden freedom and responsibility.

Unfortunately, a lot of these moral toddlers are popular and powerful. They will heap abuse on you if you try to live a moral life. It will confuse you and may cause you to stumble, but you need to be strong. Eventually, these children will grow up and realize you were right and they were wrong. Until then, hang in there. (365)

*Father, give me the strength to follow my own values, not those of others.*

*Avoid godless, foolish discussions
with those who oppose you with
their so-called knowledge.*

1 TIMOTHY 6:20 NLT

Young adulthood is the time to decide what you do and do not believe to be true. It's a time to question everything, reject some old things, and embrace some new things. It's a time that makes parents worry, because they know you will be looking critically at their beliefs, too.

You have to do this. You can't blindly accept everything you hear. You have to make your own decisions and be prepared to live with them or you'll be a wishy-washy nobody.

You also have to learn discernment. That's what Paul was warning Timothy about. Some positions must be taken on faith. All the talk in the world can't prove the unprovable, so look at everything carefully before you decide to embrace a stand, but realize that some things just have to be accepted on faith, not facts.

(365)

*Father, no one seems to agree on anything, including faith. Give me discernment and the courage to stand by my beliefs, even if I can't prove they are correct.*

*Perseverance must finish its work*
*so that you may be mature and complete,*
*not lacking anything.*

JAMES 1:4

We don't often think of perseverance as a blessing or something beneficial to our growth. We persevere because the only other options are defeat or retreat. We don't go out looking for the chance to persevere; it usually involves unpleasant experiences.

Whether or not we want these experiences, they will come. The requirements of our job may be beyond our capabilities, yet we persevere and eventually learn how to handle the work. Losing the twenty pounds we put on at college seems to go on forever, yet we lose a little every week and eventually get there.

Perseverance is tiny little steps toward a goal, not one valiant effort that solves the problem immediately. It teaches patience, planning, and working for future rewards instead of instant gratification—all things that lead to maturity and completeness.

**(365)**

*Father, perseverance is hard work, no matter what the goal is. Give me the patience and foresight I need to persevere and mature.*

*And we know that in all things God works*
*for the good of those who love him,*
*who have been called according to his purpose.*

ROMANS 8:28

I guess we're just going to have to Romans 8:28 this," Jack's pastor commented when he faced troubles. Jack liked the expression and knew immediately what Pastor Steve meant. They were just going to have to trust that God knew what He was doing and that He remained in control. In the end, God would bring good out of the worst situation.

Are you in a situation that needs Romans 8:28ing? Maybe you just lost your job because of company downsizing. Or your plans for more schooling fell through. Can you trust God for His timing? Maybe He has a better job that you never would have looked for otherwise. Perhaps there's a different type of schooling in your future. Wait for Him, and He'll show you the way.

When troubles come calling, trust the God who can work anything out for people whom He's called to serve Him. He has a plan for each believer's life.

Are you following that plan today?

**365**

*Lord, I know Your plan is best for my future. Help me walk in it hour by hour.*

*Catch for us the foxes,*
*the little foxes that ruin the vineyards,*
*our vineyards that are in bloom.*

SONG OF SONGS 2:15

Leave your dirty dishes overnight, and what could have been an easy cleaning job becomes a crusty, dried-on mess. Don't do them in the morning, and their smell could soon drive you from your home.

Sin is like those dishes. Deal with it when you first notice it in your life, and it doesn't get ingrained. You confess it to God, turn away from it quickly, and like the little fox mentioned in Song of Songs, it won't become a big fox that ruins the fruit in your spiritual vineyard.

Ignore sin until it has a real hold on you, and your vines start dying.

Are you bearing a grudge, ignoring a task God has set before you, or losing sight of your daily walk with God? Act today. Move that little fox out of your spiritual life and into the forest, where it belongs.

**365**

*Lord, I don't want sin growing in my life instead of Your fruit of the Spirit. Rid me of unforgiven sin.*

*We all stumble in many ways.*
*If anyone is never at fault in what he says,*
*he is a perfect man,*
*able to keep his whole body in check.*

JAMES 3:2

Can you imagine never saying the wrong thing? Never telling even the whitest of lies. Not embarrassing someone by saying something clumsy. Teaching the Word and getting everything right.

Life would be just about perfect if you could get your tongue under control.

That's what Scripture says. You see, what you say reflects all the things you're thinking and feeling. It shows who you really are.

Maybe we Christians have less trouble with our mouths than a coworker who swears constantly or someone who has low self-esteem and always berates herself. But perfect?

Only Jesus is truly perfect. He never gave bad advice or unintentionally hurt someone. Sometimes He told the painful truth as a warning to sinners, but He was never mean.

Need to know what to say or how to say it? Look toward Jesus. Though you may still make mistakes, you'll draw closer to His contagious perfection every day.

*O Perfect One, I want to be nearby, to catch more of Your nature every day.*

55

*Rejoice in the LORD your God,*
*for he has given you the autumn rains in righteousness.*
*He sends you abundant showers,*
*both autumn and spring rains, as before.*

JOEL 2:23

Most of us can stay dry if we want to. It's a luxury a lot of people don't have, though. And although a drought will raise supermarket prices, few of us will ever face starvation. We can pretty much avoid the downside of the weather nowadays.

Fortunately, God is good with the details of life. We don't really care if it rains on a given day or not, but He knows better and faithfully provides rain when it's needed. It's such a little detail to us that you'd think He would delegate it to someone else, but He hangs on to the responsibility and takes care of it for us. If He's faithful in this matter, imagine how faithful He is in everything else.

**⟨365⟩**

*Father, thank You for the rain that falls and keeps the world in bloom. Only You know how all the parts of this world fit together and how to make it work the way You designed it.*

*"Let your light shine before men,
that they may see your good deeds
and praise your Father in heaven."*

MATTHEW 5:16

If you are going to do good deeds, it's a good idea to be sure of your motivation. Are you secretly doing them for your own reputation or pleasure, or are you doing them for the glory of God?

Although doing good deeds involves action on your part, the greater portion of them also involves inaction. A light doesn't shine for its own glory. It just sits there and glows, showing the actions of others, just like a mirror doesn't physically do anything but reflect the actions of others.

In the same way, good deeds should show and reflect the actions of God, not you. It's God who gives you the motivation to do good. Even if others see you doing the acts, what they should notice is God's love, not yours. This makes doing a simple good deed a little more complicated than you thought, but eventually you'll catch on and learn to reflect God while you stand back in the shadows.

365

*Lord, I want my actions to lead others to praise You, not me. Show me how to do this in my everyday life.*

*Blessed shalt thou be in the city,*
*and blessed shalt thou be in the field.*

DEUTERONOMY 28:3 KJV

People get locked into mental mind-sets that can strongly affect the way they look at life. Those who live in great cities consider anyone living elsewhere as hicks, narrow-minded, and somewhat slow, both physically and mentally. Those living in small towns think all city dwellers are heartless, cold, and narrow-minded. City folk transformed into country folk say they are never accepted in their new homes, while those who move from the country to the city say the exact same thing.

Nothing is ever going to change this. We can always find someone to look down on, and even though the Bible warns us not to act this way, it still goes on.

What we continue to forget is that God really doesn't care where we live. To Him, it's how we live that counts, and we can live a blessed life anywhere we want to. Good people can live in cities or towns; bad people can live on farms or in condos. It's not the place that counts; it's the hearts living there.

**365**

*Father, teach me not to judge people on the basis of where they live, but to accept everyone as a potential child of God.*

*Make it your ambition to lead a quiet life,*
*to mind your own business*
*and to work with your hands. . .*
*so that your daily life may win the respect of outsiders*
*and so that you will not be dependent on anybody.*

1 THESSALONIANS 4:11–12

These verses summarize the aim of all education: to be able to take care of yourself when you go out into the world. They also tell you how to act when you're supporting yourself while furthering your education: Lead a quiet life, mind your own business, and do your work.

Assignments, term papers, and demanding teachers will pretty much see to it that you lead a quiet life—relatively speaking, that is. If you're trying to balance work while getting a higher degree, you need to strike a delicate balance between work and relaxation. One way or another, the work has to get done, but you do need to take time for fun. This is a balance you need to find with God's help.

**365**

*Father, help me figure out how to get everything done and still have some time to enjoy myself.*

*Cast all your anxiety on him*
*because he cares for you.*

1 PETER 5:7

Have you discovered the difference between fear and anxiety yet? They're not the same. For one thing, fear is productive. Fear is that heart-thumping moment when you know it could all be over. The car that appears over the hill while you're passing another car causes a stab of fear, which in turn gets you back into the right-hand lane as fast as possible. Fear can be dealt with by an action you can take. Most of the time, fear helps you save yourself.

Anxiety is never productive. There is no immediate danger in sight, just a vague, overpowering feeling of impending disaster. Anxiety over car accidents may keep you out of cars, but it never teaches you to be a good driver. Anxiety paralyzes you, takes you out of the action altogether. It's a useless emotion that cripples a perfectly good life.

The Bible tells us to shun anxiety, to throw it all on God. There's enough in the world that deserves our fear, but nothing in the world should make us anxious.

**365**

*Father, when anxiety takes hold of me and paralyzes me, teach me to give it over to You.*

*Apply your heart to instruction and
your ears to words of knowledge.*

PROVERBS 23:12

Everyone looks back on high school and college days as days of carefree fun. Of course, that's because additional cares and responsibilities follow the school years, and sometimes catching the 7:00 a.m. train makes sitting in a classroom seem like a piece of cake.

The truth is, learning is hard work. It's not half as carefree as we remember it being. Names, dates, equations, philosophies, term papers, and unreasonably high grade curves give students a lot of grief. All that knowledge doesn't just flow into your brain and stick. If you're juggling course work for a higher degree with work responsibilities, you're probably realizing that fact all over again.

Don't be discouraged, though. No matter what challenges life brings you, your heavenly Father is always by your side, waiting to help you out.

$365$

*Father, remind me today that nothing is too hard for me
when You are by my side.*

*For our backsliding is great;*
*we have sinned against you.*

JEREMIAH 14:7

C hoosing the moral way certainly leads to an interesting life. One day, you feel that you've got it down pat. You know where you're going and are zipping right along on the highway to heaven. The next day, you're up to your axles in mud, going nowhere at all or being towed back to some intersection you passed years ago.

Backsliding is a devastating experience. You'd licked that problem. There were plenty of others to work on, but that particular one was behind you forever (you thought). But there it is again, standing in the middle of the road and mocking you. Maybe it'll be easier to get past it this time, but what a waste of effort.

Even when we know that God has forgiven our sins, we still get angry at our failures. They hurt our egos. When we backslide, however, the only thing we can do is confess our failure, accept God's forgiveness, and get back on the road again. It's a long journey, and there's no point in wallowing in the mud.

(365)

*Father, thank You for Your forgiveness when I lose my way. I can never be the person I want to be without Your help and encouragement.*

*For the word of God is living and active.*
*Sharper than any double-edged sword,*
*it penetrates even to dividing soul and spirit,*
*joints and marrow;*
*it judges the thoughts and attitudes of the heart.*

HEBREWS 4:12

Have you ever picked up your devotional, read the Scripture, and felt as if God had written that verse especially for you? It went right to your heart because you were living out that verse.

The Bible isn't like any other book. Though you might enjoy a novel or learn a lot from a how-to book, neither reaches deep inside your soul the way Scripture does. The Word of God gets straight inside you and cuts to the truth in an instant. The Spirit can wield it like a sword, cutting sin out of your life.

But you have to hold still while God uses that sword; otherwise you can get all cut up. You'll leave a painful quiet time without the benefit of having the cancer of sin removed. Let God have His way with you, and though the sword might hurt at first, healing can come rapidly.

By the end of your prayers, you might feel whole again.

*Holy Spirit, reach into my life with Your Word. Search out the places where sin hides, and remove it from my life.*

*Yet they cannot redeem themselves*
*from death by paying a ransom to God.*
*Redemption does not come so easily,*
*for no one can ever pay enough.*

PSALM 49:7–8 NLT

Life is so precious that not even the most wealthy person in the world could pay its real worth. Gold, paper bills, or any other financial system man has developed just can't compare to the value God places on a human being.

The Bible only speaks of One who can pay the high ransom: Jesus (Matthew 20:28). Because He was not just a man, but also God, He could pay the price. Just think. You are so valuable to God that even if someone offered Him all the wealth of the world, He would turn it down. God took only the very best for you—Jesus.

The next time someone tries to tell you you're worthless, turn to this psalm. Remember that One greater than your critic says just the opposite, and He paid the price with His Son.

### (365)

*Lord, the world is always telling me I'm not worth much.*
*Thank You for loving me more than the entire world.*

*Make sure that nobody pays back wrong for wrong,*
*but always try to be kind to each other*
*and to everyone else.*

1 THESSALONIANS 5:15

B ut you don't know what he did to me!" or, "You don't know how she hurt me!" How often people say or think these words as justification for getting back at someone who hurt them badly. The implication always follows that they have a right to retaliate. Our desire to even the score runs strong when we've been done wrong.

But it isn't the best way. When we seek our own justice, we forget how it pales before God's justice. If we leave wrongs in His hands, pray for our abusers, and wait, wonderful things can happen.

Instead of starting a long-term feud, make peace with your enemy. He may turn into a friend. But if God brings down His own justice, it will be better than yours ever could be.

Be kind to those who hurt you. Either way, you can't lose.

**365**

*Father God, thank You that Your justice is far greater than mine. When I'm wronged, let me leave the outcome of the situation in Your hands.*

*May the peoples praise you, O God. . . .*
*Then the land will yield its harvest,*
*and God, our God, will bless us.*

PSALM 67:5–6

What does praise have to do with a good harvest? Unlike the Israelites, you may not go out to a field every day to earn your living. But that doesn't mean these verses don't apply to you. The principle that as a nation our physical blessings can never exceed our spiritual blessings still works.

Worship for God shouldn't be a separate cubbyhole, completely apart from our work lives. Our spiritual attitudes spill over into the things we do every day. When we have great relationships with God, we do better at our jobs, deal better with our coworkers, and truly aid people.

The nation that worships God and tells others of His wonders will be blessed. Suddenly, the country's economy takes a turn for the better, because people are being honest with one another. Those who once fought come to agreement.

All because its inhabitants recognized their Creator.

**365**

*Lord, I praise You for the blessing You've poured out on my country. May we turn to You in praise every day.*

*He who has the Son has life;*
*he who does not have the*
*Son of God does not have life.*

1 JOHN 5:12

M any non-Christians would like to believe that
religion is a smorgasbord affair: You can take a
little here, a little there, and come up with your own
brand. Take what you like, and leave the rest behind!
All enter heaven, no matter their beliefs.

Such people have often belittled Christians for
their "narrow" idea that there is only one truth—only
those who believe in Jesus enter heaven. Even if
you're a firm believer, you may feel uncomfortable
defining a truth that leaves so many outside heaven's
gates. But you aren't being ruled by your own thinking or a nasty desire to exclude anyone. If that were
true, you'd keep the Good News to yourself.

Sure, it's easier to keep your mouth shut. But
then wouldn't you be trying to exclude others? It
would be like holding the door to heaven shut.

Are you opening heaven's door today?

**(365)**

*Jesus, I know it's not popular to tell others that You are*
*the only way to heaven. Don't let that stop me from*
*telling them the truth.*

*Who can find a virtuous woman?*
*for her price is far above rubies.*

PROVERBS 31:10 KJV

When you date someone, do you look for the best-looking girl around, the guy with the most money—or a person with good character?

Dreams of your future spouse probably include a great-looking person, romantic evenings together, and wonderful conversations. You may not imagine a man who's truthful or a woman who treats her parents with respect.

God doesn't say you can't marry a good-looking mate or even one with a hefty bank account. But you could live without them. You can't live happily with a weak character.

Character doesn't look glamorous. You can't show off by sending your friend a picture of it. But you can live with it for a happy lifetime. You'll never worry where your mate is when you know he's trustworthy. You'll never fear a family get-together when you know she'll treat your parents kindly.

Is your date a noble character—or just a character?

{365}

*Lord, character may not be the asset I'm dreaming of, but I know it's important. Turn my heart toward someone with a strong love for You and the willingness to do right.*

> *"Only in his hometown, among his relatives and in his own house is a prophet without honor."*

MARK 6:4

If you're the first in your family to know Jesus, instead of just religion, you may have days when you get in heated discussions, hear all kinds of accusations, and almost wish you'd never been the one God called.

Breaking new ground for Jesus is tough. Everyone—even a non-Christian—holds his spiritual beliefs firmly and with strong emotion. Sometimes Satan has a strong hold on people, and they struggle when they hear the truth.

When your siblings aren't polite about their thoughts on your faith, your parents ignore your witness, or your cousin says, "It's just a stage you're going through," stand firm. Even Jesus didn't get everyone to listen to Him, and the Old Testament prophets got more abuse than you probably ever will.

The witness still goes on, and people come to Jesus every day. Maybe soon it will be that cousin who belittled you.

(365)

*Lord, I need to trust in You, even when people don't listen to my words. Keep me firm in faith, and give me the words You'd have me share with them.*

*I praise you because I am*
*fearfully and wonderfully made;*
*your works are wonderful.*

PSALM 139:14

If all humanity worked for years on it, we'd never create a wonder like the human body. Imagine designing various body-part cells, each working smoothly and reproducing its very own sort. How much time would it take to make every atom of a healthy body work in sync with the others?

God created all this—and more—just out of His head. No laboratory, no special equipment; the Creator's mind alone worked it out in amazing detail, made it, and set this "invention" in an equally marvelous world.

When people try to tell you that everything in our universe "just happened," it's time to ask questions. Wouldn't it have taken a mighty intelligence, not just an "accident," to plan all this?

But it's not just the universe—you are wonderfully created, made to a special design, with your own fingerprints, face, and body chemistry. On top of that, God says you're wonderful.

Shouldn't something so wonderful serve Him?

**365**

*Lord, I don't think of myself as wonderful most days. I praise You for taking such care over my design. Use me for Your kingdom's business.*

*I hate double-minded men,*
*but I love your law.*

PSALM 119:113

Have you ever run into a double-minded person? It can drive you nuts!

A double-minded person believes one thing—until another person tries to sway him. Then he changes his mind. If a friend is double-minded, you'll always wonder if he will meet you when he said he will, support the cause he said he would help with, or move somewhere else on the spur of the moment. You'll never know what's up!

Double-minded people don't have a guide they follow consistently. If public opinion changes, so do they. Disapproval from a family member may sway them—today.

That's no way to live. Everyone needs to have certain standards, codes of conduct, and personal rules.

God's laws give us the guidelines we need to avoid double mindedness. When we know what's wrong, we won't do it, even if public opinion says it's right. If a friend doesn't agree with us, we'll know why we won't change our minds. We're single-minded.

365

*Lord, I don't want to sway in the breeze on every issue. Keep me firm in Your Word so I know Your laws.*

*"Shall I acquit a man with dishonest scales,
with a bag of false weights?"*

MICAH 6:11

God takes wrongdoing seriously—much more seriously than we're likely to do.

Sometimes we'd like to fudge a little. Maybe we take a box of pencils from work and excuse ourselves with the idea that we do work at home once in awhile, and we'll need them. We think we don't harm anyone if we take that little extra. We slide it behind our backs, and an hour later it doesn't bother us.

But it bothers God just as much as it bothered Him that the merchants of Judah were shortchanging customers. They used lighter weights, which meant less product for the customers and more money for them.

God is so holy that He can't ignore wrongdoing. Mismeasuring their goods was just a sign of the evil that lived in the merchants' hearts. They were more caught up in their profit than their love for God.

Don't ask God to ignore your sin. He'd be disregarding the love that's missing in your heart.

**365**

*Thank You, Lord, that You don't leave me in my sin, even when it only seems to weigh as much as a box of pencils.*

*Blessed be the LORD God of our fathers,
which hath put such a thing as this in the king's heart,
to beautify the house of the LORD which is in Jerusalem.*

Sometimes government seems out of control. You vote because you've learned that good citizens do that, but you wonder if you have any impact. As elected officials take part in evil acts, you wonder, *Is it worth it?* But if everyone who knows God steps out of the political process, wickedness only increases.

God may call you to help out the campaign of a politician with strong morality. Or you could write letters to congressional members, telling them how they should vote on an issue.

Do something else every day, too—pray. God changes the course of politics. He did that for Ezra, when King Artaxerxes, a pagan king, opened the door so that Ezra could help rebuild Jerusalem.

God can rebuild our nation, too.

**〔365〕**

*When politics seem out of control, Lord, help me to remember that everything in life is under Your control.*

> *"Speak up for those who cannot speak for themselves,*
> *for the rights of all who are destitute.*
> *Speak up and judge fairly;*
> *defend the rights of the poor and needy."*

PROVERBS 31:8–9

Jesus made it quite clear that every one of us is responsible for defending the rights of the poor and needy, but what does that mean in our everyday life? How can one person make that much difference?

We each have a vote and the responsibility to use it wisely. Where do the candidates in this election stand on human rights? What laws are they promising to make, and how will they affect the poor? What have they done in the past that foretells what they will do in the future? You don't have to make a big study of this—you'll get the drift easily enough.

There's plenty of room for differing opinions in this country, and no one should vote on the basis of only one issue, but how an election will affect the lives of the poor should be kept in mind. Compassion is never so simple as merely Republican versus Democrat.

⟨365⟩

*Father, when I vote, help me do so wisely, keeping the fate of the poor and needy in mind, no matter what my party preference may be.*

*I know how to live on almost nothing*
*or with everything.*
*I have learned the secret of living in every situation,*
*whether it is with a full stomach or empty,*
*with plenty or little.*

PHILIPPIANS 4:12 NLT

No one knows what the future will bring. Some struggle their whole lives with no visible signs of success for their efforts, while others zoom to the top and stay there. Most of us bounce around a lot, finding success in some things and failure in others.

Some people literally wish their lives away. "In six months, I'll get a raise," they say, blowing off the days between now and then as if they were unimportant. Why not have a good time in the present instead of wasting those six months? The raise may or may not come, but today is here for the taking and will never come again.

{365}

*Father, teach me not to waste any of my life while I wait for things to get better; teach me to take each day as it comes and enjoy it to the fullest.*

*"Woe to him who quarrels with his Maker."*

ISAIAH 45:9

It's a good thing this verse doesn't say, "Woe to him who complains to his Maker," or we'd all be in trouble. As it is, we often skate on pretty thin ice, because quarreling, complaining, and moaning and groaning are all a little too close for comfort.

Why doesn't God "fix" the things that are wrong in our lives?

The Bible tells us we're just the clay He works with, and how often does a pot complain to the potter? "I'd like to be a little thinner, if you don't mind." It's a stupid idea, because the potter makes what he needs, and the clay has no voice in the creation. What does the clay know about the potter's needs and plans?

In the end, we and everything else in the world are whatever God wants us to be, and arguing about it is a waste of time and energy. Be the best pot you can be, and leave the rest to the Potter.

365

*Father, I trust Your plans for me and my world. I don't know enough to argue about it, and it's not my place to do so. Forgive me when I become impatient.*

*His commands are not burdensome,*
*for everyone born of God overcomes the world.*

Suppose your doctor told you, "I can guarantee that you will live for two hundred years if you do exactly what I tell you," and then gave you a list of directions. In addition, he would give you the phone numbers of twenty people living according to his directions—all of them happily healthy and remarkably old—and these people would teach you how to follow the directions and give you all the help they could.

You'd try it, wouldn't you? But a couple of the directions would be difficult for you, even with help, and sometimes you would fail. The next time you saw the doctor, you'd confess that you had failed, expecting the worst, but the doctor would say, "That's okay. Do you still believe in me?" You'd say, "yes," and he'd say, "I forgive you. Start over."

Would you consider the doctor's directions a burden or a blessing? How does this make you feel about God's commandments and His promise of eternal life?

**365**

*Father, thank You for showing me how to live and inherit eternal life through obeying Your commands, which are not a burden, but a blessing to me.*

*So I commend the enjoyment of life,*
*because nothing is better for a man under the sun*
*than to eat and drink and be glad.*

ECCLESIASTES 8:15

You don't have to be a sourpuss to be a good Christian. There are rules and regulations that need to be attended to, but they are not meant to take the joy out of life. Just the opposite: They are meant to make life better for everyone.

Sometimes we take ourselves far too seriously, as if enjoying ourselves were a sign of weakness or a sin that would bar us from heaven. Sure, there are things forbidden to us, but much more is allowed. We don't have to drag ourselves miserably through this life in hopes of enjoying the next. What a waste that would be, what disrespect for the One who created us and our world and proclaimed them good. How can you rejoice in God and praise His name while refusing to enjoy the gifts He has given you?

**365**

*Father, thank You for all the bright and wonderful gifts You have given me. May I enjoy them with my whole heart so others will see the wonder of Your love.*

*Everyone who competes in the games
goes into strict training.
They do it to get a crown that will not last;
but we do it to get a crown that will last forever.*

1 CORINTHIANS 9:25

Do you work out to keep your body in decent shape? It takes a lot of determination and effort, but you keep at it because you know it will result in a longer, healthier life. Of course, in time your body will still fail, no matter how hard you train. There's no way around that, but you do everything you can to put it off a little longer.

What about your spiritual training? Do you give an equal amount of time and energy to that? Do you study the Bible, your spiritual training manual, and obey its commands? Do you take advantage of the personal trainers who are willing to help you at no charge? When you get in spiritual shape, do you help others with their training?

Physical training can only take you so far. Spiritual training is for eternity.

**365**

*Lord, don't let me ignore the fitness of my soul, which is far more important in the long run than the fitness of my body.*

*And be not conformed to this world:*
*but be ye transformed by the*
*renewing of your mind.*

ROMANS 12:2 KJV

The world is full of amateur tailors trying to make us fit into their patterns, even if they have to squeeze and push us into them. If we don't fit, they will claim it's not because their pattern is wrong—something's wrong with us.

Some friends think a weekend without getting drunk is a waste of time. If they can't convince you to come along, they'll find someone else to spend time with, because you obviously don't fit in.

If you've got your mind straight, this won't bother you. You wouldn't wear a pair of jeans that came up to your knees, so why should you try to be something you aren't? You're not stamped out of a mold—you're an individual with your own mind. Don't let anyone convince you that you need to conform to his or her pattern.

**(365)**

*Father, thank You for helping me set my own priorities. Give me the strength to resist those who want me to ignore my values and adopt their own.*

> *"The LORD your God is with you,*
> *he is mighty to save.*
> *He will take great delight in you,*
> *he will quiet you with his love,*
> *he will rejoice over you with singing."*

ZEPHANIAH 3:17

What's your first reaction to this verse? "Who, me?" It's a little mind-boggling, isn't it? The Lord wants to save you from your enemies, just as He did for David. He takes delight in you—you make Him smile. When you're upset, His love will calm you. And when you come to Him, He will sing a song of joy.

The Bible's not talking about a group of people, either. It's talking about you, with all your fears and all your faults. With all the billions of people in this world, all the stars in the sky, all the other forms of life here or elsewhere, God is not too busy for you. When you fall in love, God is happy with you. When you have a child, He rejoices with you. When you suffer, He suffers. When you laugh, He laughs.

How do you repay love like that? The only way you can—with love.

(365)

*Father, thank You for Your unbounded love. I know I am unworthy, but I am so grateful You care so much for me.*

*A good name is more desirable than great riches;*
*to be esteemed is better than silver or gold.*

PROVERBS 22:1

Life offers us a lot of opportunities to cheat and get away with it. Creative cheaters can bluff their way into amazing salaries, high public office, or tax refunds large enough to support a small nation, and they seem to get away with it most of the time.

When they do, it's not always because they're so clever that no one notices. Sometimes, the people around them are perfectly aware of the cheating going on—but for reasons of their own, they look the other way. But they usually know who's a cheat, and they would never trust those people with much of value.

The next time you're tempted to cheat a little, ask yourself if it's worth the consequences. What would you prefer to see on your tombstone? "Here lies an honest man," or "He was successful, but. . ."?

### (365)

*Father, there are many ways to get to the top. Help me choose the ones that earn me the respect of others, even if the path is a little longer and harder.*

> *" 'I broke the bars of your yoke*
> *and enabled you to walk with*
> *heads held high.' "*

LEVITICUS 26:13

God always wants us to walk with our heads held high, free and proud to be His children. A child of God will never be totally enslaved. The body may be captured, but inside the heart is total freedom.

Sometimes we look at people living without freedom and wonder why they put up with it. Why don't they fight back? Why don't they value themselves enough to chance a rebellion? We've been free for so long that we think "Give me liberty or give me death" is a universal sentiment.

But we don't know what's going on in the mind of another person. "Give me liberty or give me death" is a wonderful-sounding phrase, but how often have we had to back it up with the lives of our loved ones and ourselves? Others, faced with a struggle just to feed their children, may consider the phrase ridiculous. If their children survive, that's freedom enough, and they can still walk with their heads held high.

**365**

*Father, thank You for allowing me to live in a country where freedom is valued and protected. As Your child, I will always be free in my heart, no matter what the circumstances.*

*Rejoice not when thine enemy falleth,*
*and let not thine heart be glad when he stumbleth:*
*Lest the LORD see it, and it displease him,*
*and he turn away his wrath from him.*

PROVERBS 24:17–18 KJV

Here's an interesting angle on why we shouldn't clap when our enemies suffer. Our natural tendency is to be happy when the bully finally hits the playground dirt or the dictator disappears some dark night. He has gotten away with it for too long, and we rejoice when he gets his due.

But God knows the bully and the dictator. One day, His wrath will fall on them, without any help from us. He also doesn't want any cheering from the sidelines, any self-righteous gloating, any songs of joy—even ones that are hidden in our hearts. If He hears them, He will disapprove of them and turn away His wrath before the job is done. God respects everyone, good or bad, and expects us to do the same. We may not always be able to love our enemies the way God commands, but we don't have to show joy at anyone's downfall.

**365**

*Father, sometimes it's hard to respect those who don't respect me, but justice is Your job, not mine. Teach me how to love my enemies as You command.*

*Whatever you do,*
*work at it with all your heart,*
*as working for the Lord,*
*not for men, since you know*
*that you will receive an inheritance*
*from the Lord as a reward.*
*It is the Lord Christ you are serving.*

COLOSSIANS 3:23–24

Are you miserable in your job? Mentally switch employers—imagine you work for God, not your boss.

Once you decide to work as if God were your boss, everything changes. You can't call in sick every Monday when God knows every healthy cell in your body. You can't give less than your best to God, who knows exactly how capable you are and wants to reward your efforts. If it takes fifty hours a week to get the job done, would you complain to God?

A few months of this and your human supervisor is going to notice the change. You're getting the job done without resentment. Maybe you can be trusted, even promoted. She won't have the vaguest idea of what's come over you, but she'll be pleased, and supervisors who are pleased often turn into decent people. Try it.

**365**

*Father, help me do all my work as if I were working for You, no matter how bad conditions are for me.*

*Who can discern his errors?*
*Forgive my hidden faults.*

PSALM 19:12

The truth is, we all have lots of hidden faults that need confessing. Some we hide from others on purpose; some we even manage to hide from ourselves.

But God's grace is not limited by our limitations. He can see into the subconscious corners of our lives, and He can bring healing and cleansing to even those hidden dirty spots. When we can say, "Forgive me my hidden faults" and really mean it, opening ourselves to God in complete trust and surrender, then He will change us in ways we never knew we needed.

Christ offers us total forgiveness from the secret sins we hide from others, afraid they wouldn't love us if they knew what we were really like—and He also forgives the deepest sin we hide even from ourselves.

**365**

*Father, my sins are more numerous than I'll ever know, but I know Your forgiveness is complete.*

*He also told them this parable:*
*"Can a blind man lead a blind man?*
*Will they not both fall into a pit?"*

LUKE 6:39

What a delightful description Jesus gave us in this parable. You can easily see this pair ending up in a pit, because neither can see the road.

Sometimes we're no better than these foolish men. Without even thinking of it, we hang on to someone who's going in the wrong direction. By the time we realize we've been following others, not God, we're on the edge of a crater.

Want to know if you will end in a spiritual hole? Look at the people you follow. Are they filled with peace and serving God, or are they running their own show, constantly dissatisfied with life?

Since you'll end up much like the people you follow most, be sure the people you emulate are worth following. Do they do what the Bible says is right? Are they honest and loving?

In the end, make sure you're following the greatest Leader—Jesus. His paths don't go into pits.

**(365)**

*Lord, I want to be a leader who won't bring others into a pit. Guide me this day to walk in Your footsteps.*

*The Israelites ate manna forty years. . .*
*until they reached the border of Canaan.*

EXODUS 16:35

You might call it "doing laps." Just as a swimmer goes back and forth in the pool to build up strength, sometimes God keeps us in the same place, doing the same thing, for a long time.

The Israelites complained that they didn't have food, so God gave them manna. . .today and tomorrow and the next day. Boy, were they sick of that white, waferlike stuff! Like the swimmer in the pool, they never got anything different.

In our spiritual walk, when we get stuck "doing laps," we need to take a look at ourselves. Maybe, like the Israelites, we've sinned, and God is trying to humble us. Or maybe we need to gain strength, so God has us exercising the same spiritual muscle over and over again.

If you're doing laps, search your heart. Do you need to confess some sin so you can move on? If not, don't get discouraged. God is building up your strength.

That's why you're diving into the water one more time.

**(365)**

*Lord, when I feel waterlogged, show me why I'm diving into the water again.*

*Why do you boast of evil, you mighty man?*
*Why do you boast all day long,*
*you who are a disgrace in the eyes of God?*

PSALM 52:1

You're working hard, trying to be honest, even though you don't get a large salary and could really use a few things. Then a coworker boasts to someone else about a killing he made by doing wrong.

*Why him and not me?* you may wonder.

Don't follow him. First, chances are you can't duplicate what he's done. You're likely to get caught if you try to repeat the same slick deal.

But even if you could repeat his method and no one caught you, it wouldn't be worth the price. When you decided to pray, you'd feel disgrace taking up space between you and God. You'd wonder if He was listening very closely. Should you escape that quiet time without confessing the sin, you'd start feeling uncomfortable, so you'd pray less often.

Soon you wouldn't pray at all, and your church attendance would start slipping.

Don't listen to those who boast of evil; instead, do some of your own boasting in the God who saved you.

**365**

*Turn me back from sin, Lord. Close my ears to sinners' boasting.*

*"Let God weigh me in honest scales
and he will know that I am blameless."*

JOB 31:6

Job seemed to have everything—a happy family, lots of money, and a great relationship with God. Who wouldn't envy him?

Until disaster struck.

Suddenly Job was scratching his sores, sitting atop a dunghill, without a supportive family—and with friends like his, no one needed an enemy! Where had Job gone wrong? Hadn't he been honest with everyone he'd dealt with? He hadn't made his millions by walking over others. This honest man cried out to God.

But God didn't seem to answer.

We know. We've tried our best at work, but we get laid off. We're honest with our money, but someone else takes his girl to a play, while we go to the park. We pray, but nothing changes.

Has God forgotten us? No way! The answer may not come overnight—it didn't for Job. But in the end, blessing overwhelmed him. God does that for us, too. Sometimes, the more time He takes to develop a blessing, the better it is.

365

*When Your blessings come slowly, keep me patient, Lord.*

*Thou shalt neither vex a stranger,*
*nor oppress him:*
*for ye were strangers in the land of Egypt.*

EXODUS 22:21 KJV

You move to a new town or a new school, and for the first few days you feel really strange. You don't know where to go for anything you need. You don't know whom to ask for advice.

Then someone comes along and tells you about some good stores, the best bank, and maybe a great doctor. All of a sudden, you're beginning to find your feet. You feel more secure, and life balances out again.

God knows what it feels like to be in a strange place (after all, didn't Jesus leave His home to come to earth?). He understands that sometimes you have to go to a new place (didn't He call Abram to move?).

Maybe because of that, He tells us to have compassion for the new person on the block. We don't need to wonder if we should stretch out a welcoming hand. God has been there before us, greeting the outcast.

**(365)**

*Thank You, Lord, for caring for me when I'm in a new place. Help me to reach out to others who are feeling strange in a new town, a new job, or a new country.*

*A man's wisdom gives him patience; it
is to his glory to overlook an offense.*

Ever gotten stuck at an airport? Maybe your flight gets canceled—or you drive in to pick up a family member or friend and see *delayed* in the place of an arrival time.

Either way, you're stuck. The only decision you really can make is how you'll handle the situation. Will you gripe and complain until everyone within a ten-foot radius decides to "get something to eat"? Or will you make use of your time by catching up on reading, praying, or making a new friend of a fellow traveler?

We can't always control life, but we can take charge of our reaction to it. Gripers don't enjoy those hours of their lives, but those who learn a new skill, draw closer to God, or share life with someone new can feel blessed.

**365**

*Though self-control doesn't always come easy to me, Lord, I know it's part of the fruit of Your Spirit. When I have to wait, help me to bear a good crop for You.*

*"For God so loved the world that
he gave his one and only Son,
that whoever believes in him shall
not perish but have eternal life."*

JOHN 3:16

Eternal life"—have you ever thought of time without end, stretching on and on? But not dull, useless hours or overly hectic days—time for God's kind
of life that's continually fresh and exciting without
being rushed.

Most of us can rattle off John 3:16 without even
thinking about it. But have we thought about what
we'll do with endless life with the Creator of the
universe?

If we listed everything we'd like to do in heaven,
most of us would have trouble filling up a month,
much less eternity. From an earthly point of view, we
can imagine boredom setting in early.

But living in the home of "new life" leaves no room
for boredom. Scripture only gives us faint glimpses,
but certainly a Father who took such efforts to save us
wouldn't skimp on our shared eternity.

No matter what we do in heaven, God will be
bigger than our wildest dreams.

〔365〕

*Lord, when I think of time without limits, my mind goes
fuzzy. I only know I want to glorify You with every
atom of my being.*

*For that ye ought to say,*
*If the Lord will, we shall live,*
*and do this, or that.*

JAMES 4:15 KJV

What does James mean in this verse?" Kirsten asked. "Sounds as if he's saying we should never make plans. If I did that, my life'd be a mess!"

Her Bible study leader explained that God wasn't frowning on our making plans. But He doesn't want us to get caught up in our plans and never look to Him for guidance. Planning done without God leads down a dead-end street.

As the end of the year nears, you're looking forward to 365 new days filled with career and personal opportunities. Maybe lots of options vie for your attention: Should you move in with friends, take a job in another state, or start dating someone new?

Though you see the exciting changes ahead, you don't have a God's-eye view of your life. He sees the big picture and wants to help you make the right choices.

So why not ask Him what the next step is?

(365)

*This new year needs to be filled, Lord. Let it overflow*
*with Your will for me.*

*The evil deeds of a wicked man ensnare him;*
*the cords of his sin hold him fast.*
*He will die for lack of discipline,*
*led astray by his own great folly.*

PROVERBS 5:22–23

Tie a puppy out on a leash, and you're bound to come back a few minutes later and find her all wrapped up in her own cord. Though she didn't mean to get in trouble, she is, and she can't untie herself to get free.

That's the way sin wraps people up. They're playing at life, doing all the things they enjoy, and taking no heed of the way they're getting tied up in wrongdoing. Once they're held fast, the only one who can free them is God.

Even once you know Him, it takes discipline to avoid getting tied up in sin. Instead of foolishly walking down a road of ease, keep an eye on where you're heading. Maybe you need to make some lifestyle changes.

Don't scratch every party off your schedule, but balance your free time by helping out at church, doing a favor for a neighbor, or spending time in serious Bible study. Make your free time count for Christ.

〈365〉

*Every moment of my life is Yours, Jesus. Help me make each one count for You.*